LOVE
My Search for Truth

Annie

Illustrated by Rachelle Rouse

VANTAGE PRESS
New York

Acknowledgements

Literary Agent J.T. O'Hara
Editor Richard Showstack
(J. T. O'Hara and Associates)

Elizanda M. de la Sota, Ph.D.

Elizabeth Pomada. Dorka Podmajersky.
Orville R. Blum. Diana George, LMSW-ACP.
Sister Mary Ana of the Divine Mercy. Karen Menzie.

Because you are who you are,
the manuscript is now a book.
Because you are who you are,
the book is as it is.
Thank you for believing in me.
Thank you for your help.

FIRST EDITION

All rights reserved, including the right of
reproduction in whole or in part in any form.

Copyright © 2003 by Annie

Published by Vantage Press, Inc.
516 West 34th Street, New York, New York 10001

Manufactured in the United States of America
ISBN: 0-533-14554-6

Library of Congress Catalog Card No.: 2003091184

0 9 8 7 6 5 4

Dedicated

To the man who has been
the single-most influence
of love in my life.
To my adult son

Scott

Preface

In December 1999, I was driving my usual forty minute commute to work when the words "love, thoughts to ponder" came to mind. My immediate reaction was to think, "That sounds like the title of a book." The words stayed with me throughout the day. When I arrived home that evening I got out paper and pencil and wrote them down: *love, thoughts to ponder.*

During that evening and during the course of my normal daily routine for the next two weeks, one thought after another simply and wonderfully occurred to me. The thoughts were so striking to me that as I thought of them, I wrote them down on napkins, on receipts, on the back of bank deposit slips, on anything available. At the end of each day I typed them into the word processor in the order the thoughts occurred to me.

The next two and a half years were spent in search of a publisher. At some point during those two and a half years I questioned why I was having such a difficult time finding the means to publish. It seemed to me that the writing was inspired, and as it was inspired then the doors should be opening to me and it should be published. Why was I receiving rejection after rejection? Why didn't a publisher jump at the opportunity to print my manuscript? What was wrong with the publishing world? What was the hang-up?

Even as I asked these questions, I knew the answer. The manuscript was indeed ready for publication. It was I, Annie, who was not ready. I had written a series of statements about love. Each statement rang of truth to me and yet I had no idea, I did not understand, what I had written.

It is now July of 2002. What has changed? I have changed. I still cannot honestly say that I fully understand what I have written, but I can say that I have written a kind of journal of *my search for truth.*

I have come to understand that each of us, each person now living and breathing, is on an earthly journey. I have come to understand that I am not responsible for anyone else's journey. I am only responsible for my journey. And I have come to understand that my journey is about the exploration and discovery of the meaning of love.

It has been said that, "The greatest sign of intimacy is our willingness to share our search for God." It is with that thought in mind that I now share this book with you. I share with you the deepest yearning of my soul: my yearning for love, my yearning for God. . . .

I offer you this book
with love,
Annie

To love is to go where your heart leads.

It is okay to feel

the reality of love

in all things

at all times.

Love

survives

death.

Love

is equally available

to all.

Love

in and of itself

is prayer.

If you cannot find happiness,

search for peace.

If you search for peace,

you will find love.

When seen through the eyes of love, all things make sense.

It is difficult to comprehend

but at this very moment,

because of the reality of love,

all things are

just as they are meant to be.

Love knows no limits.

Love

without

ceasing.

Do not be afraid to be alone

in silence with yourself,

for that is where

you will best find love.

In a heart filled with love,

there is no room for pettiness.

God is love.

Love is God.

Denial of the past

is denial

of one of the greatest

avenues of love.

Meaning
can only be found
through the filter
of love.

To love

is the easiest thing

on this earth to do.

To love

is the most difficult thing

on this earth to do.

Why keep love secret

We are free to love.

Or not.

Do not be in a hurry to find love.

Just be vigilant.

Yahweh. Jesus. Buddha.

Allah. Krishna. Etc.

The message is the same.

The message is love.

Only

love

can fill the void.

Let go of pride.

Make room for love.

When you have

nothing to think about,

think about love.

When you have

too much to think about,

think only about love.

What a warm blanket love is!

What a cool breeze love is!

Can you think

of a joy

greater than

love?

To love

is to listen.

To be loved

is to be listened to.

Love

never

stops.

To acknowledge the reality of love is to acknowledge the reality of God.

The source of all inspiration

is either love

or

lack of love.

There is no such thing

as a heart

without love.

If you listen

you will hear the music

of love.

I am lovable.

You are lovable.

There is nothing so simple

or so complex as love.

Start with the simple.

Fantasy conceived in love

    is a coping device

not to be discouraged.

Experience love.

Experience God.

Love is

    where you would least expect it.

Love comes

    when you would least expect it.

Love

gives reason

to pain.

Love accepts me

as I am.

Love accepts others

as they are.

When in doubt

think in terms of love.

Sometimes it is easier

to love someone

than to like them.

Can there ever be

too

much

love?

Love is timeless.

Love is everywhere.

Love is our link to the divine.

Look

inward.

Find the place

where love dwells.

Enjoy love.

Celebrate love.

All things

work

for the good

of one

who loves.

Use the love prayer.

The benefits

are multitudinous.

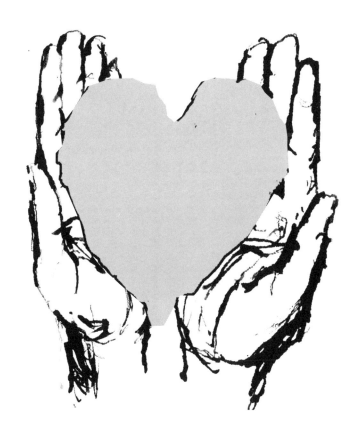

Love

rankles

against

injustice.

It is important

that you love yourself.

You know you love yourself when

you allow others to love you.

Love is gentle.

Love is kind.

But love is not fragile.

Everyone loves

differently

and

uniquely.

You can see

love

but only

if you are looking

for it.

Love

waits patiently.

Work is not a burden

when done with love.

When someone says,

"Pray for me,"

they are asking you

to love them.

Love gives.

        Love receives.

    Unconditionally.

Love protects us.

Love today.

Tomorrow will take care of itself.

Love is full

of many wonder-filled surprises.

Banish fear.

Welcome love.

Love

is nourishment

for the soul.

Love maturely--like a child.

Our only need

is

to give

and

to receive

love.

Love is human.

Love is divine.

Only in love

will the soul

find rest.

Use the word "love"

with fore-thought.

If we allow it,

love

will show us the way.

Wisdom is love's truth.

Love

is

our life's purpose.

Hate

is

lack of love.

The greatest lessons
of love can be learned
through the pain
of our mistakes.

Busy-ness wards off love.

Relax.

Enjoy life.

Love can guide us

out of any dilemma.

Even if it led us there.

To love

is

to take risks.

Believe and remember:

love never fails.

Love intensely—

as if

this were your first day to love

and

your last day to love.

Volunteer your love.

Love was and is forever.

Love—a glorious mystery.

Each person

is responsible

for his or her own

love life.

Sex without intimacy is just sex.

Sex with intimacy is love-making.

When said with love,

painful truths

can be heard.

Allow yourself to sink into the unfathomable depths of love.

Allow yourself to rise to the unfathomable heights of love.

Do not be afraid.

Open your mind and heart

to love.

To love is to forgive myself.

To love is to accept that others will either forgive me or not forgive me.

Sometimes

we have to suffer in silence.

To endure silent suffering

in the name of love

is a powerful prayer.

To love

is to say hello.

To love

is to say good-bye.

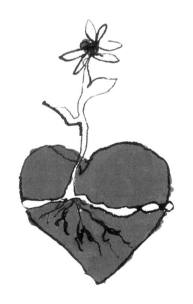

Miracles occur

in the silence

of the heart.

Love gives us strength

to concede when we are wrong.

It is,

    perhaps,

more difficult

to receive love

than to give love.

It is never too late to love.

Never underestimate the power of love.

Smile the smile

of one who knows love.

No wrong is so great

that it cannot be healed

by love.

If you do not like someone consider how they love differently from you.

To judge

another person's way of love

as "right" or "wrong"

is to judge

oneself.

The common bond

between and among

all mankind

is love.

Yahweh is to a Jew

as Jesus is to a Christian

as Buddha is to a Buddhist

as Allah is to a Muslim.

Love encompasses all.

Each person's love-journey is *their* love-journey.

A smile.

A handshake.

A kind word.

A hug.

Oh, the power of love!

Even if hidden, love can be found in honesty.

If you help the helpless,

help them with love.

If you donate a dollar,

donate with love.

If you donate a million dollars,

donate with love.

Love knows

      no barriers

      of distance.

Love knows

      no barriers

      of time.

Why are we afraid

to tell our friends

that

we love them?

Why are we afraid

to love

the universe

and all that dwell in it?

Invite and welcome love into your mind and heart and soul.

Do not be afraid.

Ask love to come.

The Golden Rule

Buddhism: Hurt not others with that whichs pains yourself. *Udanavarga 5.18.*

Christianity: Always treat others as you would like them to treat you; that is the Law and the Prophets. *Bible, Matthew 7:12.*

Confucianism: Do not unto others what you would not they should do unto you. *Analects 15:23.*

Hinduism: This is the sum of duty: Do nothing to others which if done to you would cause you pain. *Mahabharata 5.1517.*

Islam: No one of you is a believer until he loves for his brother what he loves for himself. *Traditions.*

Jainism: In happiness and suffering, in joy and grief, we should regard all creatures as we regard our own self, and should therefore refrain from inflicting upon others such injury as would appear undesirable to us if inflicted upon ourselves. *Yogashastra 2.20.*

Judaism: What is hurtful to yourself do not to your fellow man. That is the whole of the Torah and the remainder is but commentary. Go learn it. *Talmud.*

Sikhism: As you deem yourself, so deem others. Then you will become a partner in partnership to heaven. *Kabir.*

Taoism: Regard your neighbor's loss as your own loss. *T'ai shang kan ying p'ien.*

About the Author

ANNIE wholeheartedly supports the good works of non-profit agencies. She has committed a portion of her income from sales of *Love: My Search for Truth* to several non-profit agencies of her choice.

The author was raised in Amarillo, Texas. She now lives in Bastrop, a small, friendly town near Austin and San Antonio. Annie has a master's degree in professional counseling and has worked for several non-profit agencies in the state of Texas. She has a thirty-seven-year-old son and a thirteen-year-old granddaughter. Annie enjoys collecting rare books, writing poetry, travel, yardwork and cross stitch.

About the Illustrator

Rachelle Rouse, illustrator, is a graduate of St. Edward's University in Austin with a degree in art and graphic design. She was raised in Halletsville, Texas. She now lives and works in Austin.